ADVANCED PALMISTRY: UNLOCKING HIDDEN SIGNS, RARE MARKINGS & KARMIC PATTERNS (VOL. II)

FROM THE AUTHOR TO THE READER:

WHY YOU SHOULD READ VOLUME I & VOLUME II FOR A COMPLETE UNDERSTANDING OF PALMISTRY

Dear Reader,

Thank you for embarking on this fascinating journey into the world of palmistry! Whether you are a curious beginner or someone eager to master the art of hand reading, I have carefully designed **Volume I and Volume II** to provide you with a **step-by-step learning experience** that builds from fundamental principles to advanced techniques.

WHY READ VOLUME I?

"Palmistry for Beginners: The Ultimate Guide to Reading Palms & Decoding Your Destiny" (Vol. 1) introduces you to the **foundations of palmistry** in a structured, easy-to-understand manner. In this book, you will learn:

✔ The history and significance of palmistry
✔ The four hand shapes and what they reveal about personality
✔ The major palm lines (Life Line, Heart Line, Head Line, and Fate Line) and their meanings
✔ How to read palms step by step with a beginner-friendly approach
✔ Common myths and misconceptions about palmistry

If you're new to palmistry, **Volume I is the perfect starting point**—helping you build a strong foundation before diving into more advanced interpretations.

WHY CONTINUE WITH VOLUME II?

"Advanced Palmistry: Unlocking Hidden Signs, Rare Markings & Karmic Patterns" (Vol. 2) takes you deeper into the **mystical and rare aspects of hand reading**. In this book, you will discover:

✔ Special and secondary lines, including the Sun Line, Marriage Line, and Travel Lines
✔ The hidden markings and signs that indicate fame, wealth, and past-life karma
✔ Advanced techniques for reading mounts, finger shapes, and nail structures
✔ How palmistry connects with intuition, astrology, and spiritual growth
✔ Real-life case studies to enhance your interpretation skills

While **Volume I gives you the tools to start reading palms, Volume II enhances your ability to uncover deeper, more personalized insights**—perfect for those who want to **move beyond basics and truly master palmistry**.

THE COMPLETE LEARNING EXPERIENCE

By reading **both volumes**, you will develop **a well-rounded understanding** of palmistry—from the simplest concepts to the most **intricate and mystical** interpretations. Each book complements the other, ensuring that you

progress naturally and confidently in your palmistry journey.

I hope these books **inspire you, empower you, and help you unlock the wisdom hidden in the palms of your hands!**

Happy Reading & Palm Reading!

**Warm regards,
- Nabanita Chakraborty**

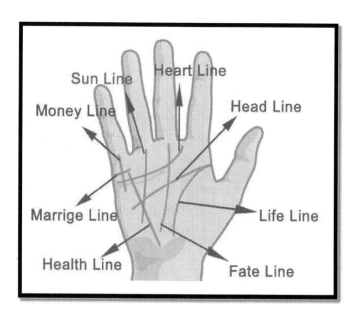

TABLE OF CONTENTS

INTRODUCTION

- How This Volume Expands on Volume 1
- What You'll Learn in Advanced Palmistry

CHAPTER 1: THE MOUNTS OF THE HAND – PERSONALITY TRAITS & STRENGTHS

- The Seven Major Mounts & Their Meanings
- How to Identify Strong & Weak Mounts
- What It Means If a Mount is Too Prominent or Flat

CHAPTER 2: MARKINGS ON THE PALM – HIDDEN MESSAGES

- Transverse Lines, Tridents, Tassels, Breaks, Chains
- Upward & Downward Lines – Positive & Negative Influences
- Squares, Stars, Crosses – Protection & Challenges
- Fish Sign – Spiritual Growth & Unexpected Success
- Simian Line – Intense Focus & Emotional Extremes
- Mole Interpretation on the Palm – Significance of Placement

CHAPTER 3: FINGERPRINTS & SKIN TEXTURE – HIDDEN CLUES IN YOUR HANDS

- Dermatoglyphics: The Study of Fingerprints
- Loop, Whorl, and Arch Patterns & Their Meanings
- How Skin Texture Reflects Mental & Emotional State

CHAPTER 4: PALMISTRY & CHAKRAS – THE ENERGY CONNECTION

- How Hand Lines Relate to Energy Centers
- The Role of Chakras in Palm Readings
- Healing & Strengthening Chakras Through Palmistry

CHAPTER 5: THE SCIENCE VS. SPIRITUALITY OF PALMISTRY

- How Modern Science Views Palmistry
- The Role of Intuition in Palm Reading
- Palmistry vs. Numerology vs. Vedic Astrology – A Comparative Analysis

CHAPTER 6: PALMISTRY CHARTS FOR ADVANCED READERS

- Hand Shapes, Fingerprints & Line Charts
- Special Symbols & Their Interpretations

CHAPTER 7: HANDWRITING & PALMISTRY – A SURPRISING CONNECTION

- How Handwriting Reflects Personality
- Finger Flexibility & Writing Pressure – Hidden Clues

- Similarities Between Palmistry & Graphology

CONCLUSION

- How to Continue Your Journey in Palmistry
- Practicing Ethical & Responsible Palm Reading
- The Future of Palmistry in the Modern World

INTRODUCTION

HOW THIS VOLUME EXPANDS ON VOLUME 1

If you have read **Volume 1: "Palmistry for Beginners: The Ultimate Guide to Reading Palms & Decoding Your Destiny"**, you already have a strong foundation in palm reading. You've learned about the **major palm lines, hand shapes, and the step-by-step process of interpreting a palm**. You now understand how to decode a person's basic personality traits, emotional patterns, career tendencies, and life direction by analyzing their hands.

However, palmistry goes far beyond just the basics. While **Volume 1** provided you with the essential tools, **this volume is designed to take you deeper**—unlocking the **hidden signs, rare markings, karmic influences, and intuitive interpretations** that can transform your palmistry skills from beginner to advanced.

In **Volume 2**, we will go beyond general meanings and explore **how subtle details in the hands can reveal profound life insights**. This book is for those who want to go from simply "reading palms" to truly **understanding the soul's journey through the hands**.

WHAT YOU'LL LEARN IN ADVANCED PALMISTRY

- **Rare and Hidden Markings** – Discover unique signs like the Mystic Cross, Healer's Mark, and Money Triangle, which indicate special abilities and life influences.
- **Secondary & Special Lines** – Learn how the **Sun Line, Marriage Line, Health Line, and Travel Lines** provide deeper insights into fame, love, well-being, and life changes.
- **Mounts of the Palm** – Understand how the raised areas of the palm (Mounts of Jupiter, Saturn, Apollo, Mercury, etc.) reveal strengths, weaknesses, and life experiences.
- **Fingers & Their Symbolism** – Decode personality and fate through finger length, shape, and flexibility.
- **Intuitive Palmistry & Karmic Signs** – Learn how the hands reflect **past life karma, destiny patterns, and spiritual growth**.
- **Case Studies & Practical Readings** – Study real-life examples to enhance your ability to make **accurate, meaningful interpretations**.

This volume will not only enhance your technical skills but also **deepen your intuitive understanding of palmistry**. By the time you complete this book, you'll be able to read hands with greater accuracy, uncover hidden details that most beginners miss, and even use palmistry as a tool for **guiding others in their life path**.

Let's begin your journey into Advanced Palmistry!

PART 1: ADVANCED TECHNIQUES IN PALMISTRY

CHAPTER 1: THE MOUNTS OF THE HAND – PERSONALITY TRAITS & STRENGTHS

Palmistry is not just about reading lines; the **mounts of the hand** play a crucial role in understanding a person's personality, strengths, and even life experiences. These mounts are the **raised areas or fleshy pads** found at the base of the fingers and other parts of the palm. Each mount is linked to a specific planet, which governs different aspects of life, such as intelligence, emotions, creativity, ambition, and communication.

By analyzing the **size, shape, firmness, and prominence** of these mounts, you can determine a person's **natural talents, weaknesses, and potential life challenges**.

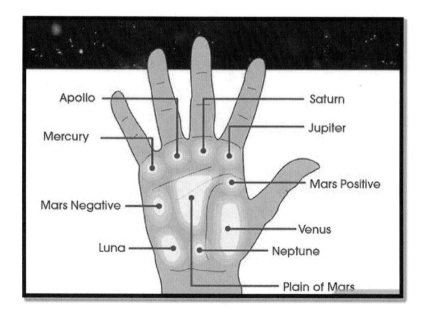

THE SEVEN MAJOR MOUNTS & THEIR MEANINGS

In palmistry, there are seven key mounts, each representing a celestial body and its associated personality traits:

1. MOUNT OF JUPITER (BELOW THE INDEX FINGER – LEADERSHIP & AMBITION)

- A strong Mount of Jupiter indicates **confidence, leadership skills, and ambition**. The person is likely to be authoritative, self-motivated, and successful in careers that require power, such as politics or management.
- A weak or flat mount may suggest **a lack of confidence, low self-esteem, or difficulty in asserting oneself**.

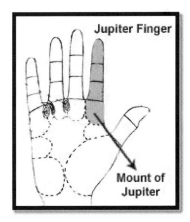

2. MOUNT OF SATURN (BELOW THE MIDDLE FINGER – WISDOM & RESPONSIBILITY)

- A prominent Mount of Saturn signifies **deep thinking, wisdom, patience, and a philosophical nature**. These individuals may be drawn to spiritual pursuits, education, or research-based careers.
- A weak mount may indicate **a lack of responsibility, fear of solitude, or difficulty in handling hardships**.

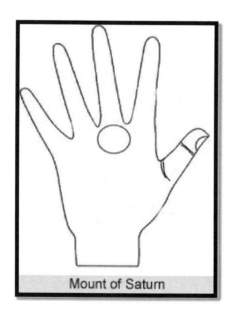

3. MOUNT OF APOLLO (BELOW THE RING FINGER – CREATIVITY & FAME)

- A well-developed Mount of Apollo represents **creativity, artistic talent, self-expression, and a love for beauty**. People with this trait are often successful in the entertainment industry, art, music, or design.
- A weak mount could suggest **a lack of confidence in showcasing talents, fear of criticism, or an unfulfilled creative side**.

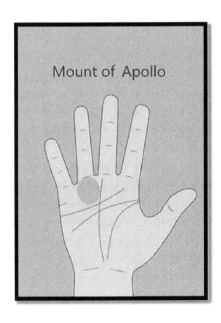

4. MOUNT OF MERCURY (BELOW THE LITTLE FINGER – COMMUNICATION & BUSINESS ACUMEN)

- If this mount is prominent, the individual is likely to be **a great communicator, a skilled negotiator, and successful in business or public speaking**. They are intelligent, quick-witted, and adaptable.
- If the mount is underdeveloped, the person may struggle with **communication, social interactions, or financial matters**.

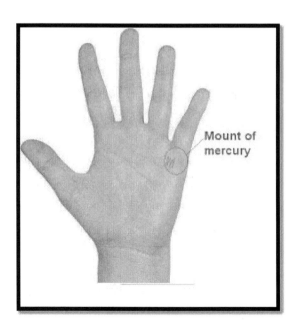

5. MOUNT OF VENUS (BELOW THE THUMB – LOVE, PASSION & RELATIONSHIPS)

- A strong Mount of Venus indicates **a passionate, romantic, and affectionate personality**. These individuals enjoy pleasures, relationships, and creative hobbies.
- A weak mount suggests **a reserved nature, difficulty expressing emotions, or a lack of passion in life**.

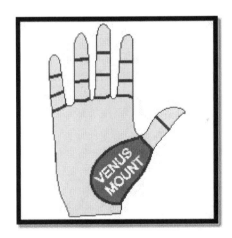

6. MOUNT OF MARS (COURAGE & RESILIENCE – TWO POSITIONS IN THE PALM)

- **Inner Mars (Near the Thumb)** – Represents **inner strength, patience, and perseverance**. A strong Inner Mars suggests emotional resilience, while a weak one may indicate emotional instability.
- **Outer Mars (Near the Little Finger)** – Represents **physical courage, aggression, and assertiveness**. A strong Outer Mars means **bravery and determination**, while a weak one suggests **fear, hesitation, or passiveness**.

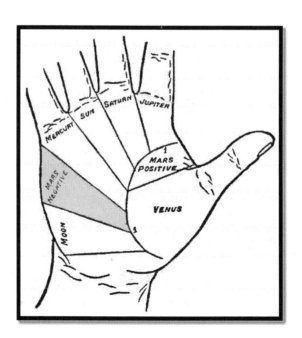

7. MOUNT OF LUNA (BELOW THE PALM'S OUTER EDGE – IMAGINATION & INTUITION)

- A prominent Mount of Luna (Moon) signifies **a strong imagination, intuition, and a deep connection with emotions**. These individuals may excel in writing, poetry, or creative fields.
- A weak mount may indicate **a lack of vision, limited imagination, or difficulty understanding emotions**.

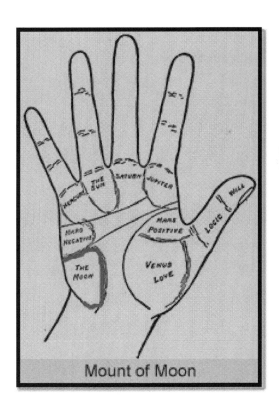

HOW TO IDENTIFY STRONG & WEAK MOUNTS

The size, texture, and **firmness** of a mount determine whether it is strong, balanced, or weak:

✔ **Strong & Well-Developed Mount** – Raised, fleshy, and firm to the touch. Indicates that the individual possesses **dominant traits associated with that mount**.

✔ **Flat or Underdeveloped Mount** – Lacks prominence, appears sunken. Suggests that the qualities linked to that mount are **less pronounced or need improvement**.

✔ **Overly Prominent or Overdeveloped Mount** – Too raised and excessively fleshy. Can indicate **exaggeration of certain traits** (e.g., an overly developed Mount of Mercury may indicate a manipulative nature).

WHAT IT MEANS IF A MOUNT IS TOO PROMINENT OR FLAT

- **An Overly Prominent Mount** – This may indicate **an excess of the planet's influence**, which can sometimes lead to negative traits.
    - Example: A **highly raised Mount of Venus** may indicate excessive indulgence in

pleasures, possessiveness in relationships, or laziness.
    - A **very strong Mount of Mars** may indicate **aggression, anger issues, or impulsiveness**.
- **A Flat or Weak Mount** – Suggests **a deficiency in that aspect of life**.
    - Example: A **flat Mount of Luna** could indicate **a lack of creativity, weak intuition, or difficulty understanding emotions**.
    - A **flat Mount of Jupiter** may suggest **low confidence, lack of leadership, or inability to take initiative**.

FINAL THOUGHTS

Understanding the mounts of the hand allows you to **read personalities, strengths, and weaknesses at a glance**. By combining this knowledge with palm lines and finger analysis, you can **create a highly accurate personality profile and even predict future tendencies**.

CHAPTER 2: MARKINGS ON THE PALM – SIGNS, SYMBOLS & THEIR MEANINGS

Palmistry goes beyond reading lines and mounts—**markings on the palm** provide valuable insights into a person's **strengths, challenges, destiny, and karmic influences**. These markings appear as **crosses, stars, islands, dots, triangles, grilles, and even moles**, each carrying a unique significance depending on its placement. Some markings indicate **good fortune and success**, while others signal **challenges, delays, or obstacles** in life.

Understanding these markings can help in providing a **detailed and accurate palm reading**. Let's explore their meanings and significance.

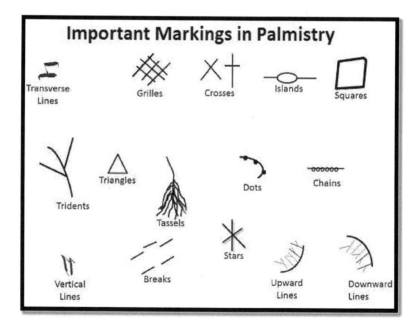

1. CROSS (X) – OBSTACLES OR TRANSFORMATION

A **cross (X-shaped mark)** can have different meanings depending on its location:

- **On the Mount of Jupiter** – Strong leadership qualities, ambition, and spiritual insight.
- **On the Head Line** – Confusion, overthinking, or mental stress.

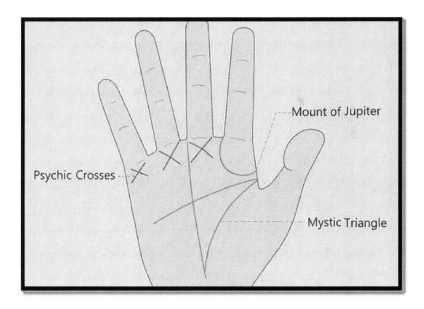

- **On the Heart Line** – Relationship troubles or emotional pain.
- **On the Mount of Saturn** – Struggles, karmic challenges, or misfortune.

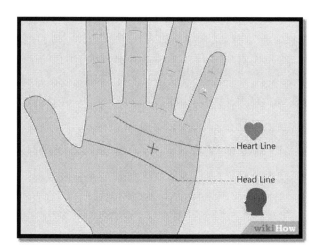

- **Between the Head Line and Heart Line (Mystic Cross)** – **Spiritual abilities, psychic gifts, and strong intuition**.

The **Mystic Cross** is a sign of **spiritual power, deep wisdom, and an intuitive mind**. If you have it, you are **blessed with divine protection and a natural connection to the unseen world**. If you don't, remember that **spiritual abilities can always be cultivated** through practice, belief, and learning.

2. STAR (★) – SUDDEN FAME & ACHIEVEMENTS

A **star marking (a clear, well-formed asterisk shape)** is a symbol of **good fortune and sudden success**:

- **On the Mount of Apollo** – Creativity, fame, and public recognition.
- **On the Mount of Jupiter** – Leadership, power, and influence.
- **On the Mount of Mercury** – Business success and intelligence.
- **On the Fate Line** – A sudden breakthrough in career or wealth.

A poorly formed star may indicate **sudden problems or setbacks** instead.

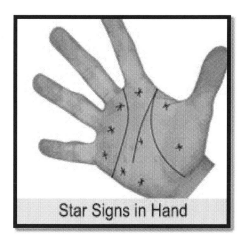
Star Signs in Hand

3. ISLAND (O) – DELAYS, CONFUSION & WEAKNESS

An **island (oval-shaped break in a line)** usually represents difficulties:

- **On the Life Line** – Health issues, emotional stress, or family problems.
- **On the Head Line** – Mental stress, confusion, or decision-making difficulties.
- **On the Heart Line** – Emotional struggles, heartbreak, or infidelity.
- **On the Fate Line** – Career instability or financial struggles.

Remedy: Meditation, positive thinking, and strengthening weak planetary influences through **gemstones or prayers**.

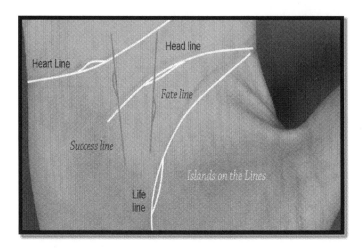

4. DOTS (•) – SUDDEN EVENTS OR SHOCKS

Dots are **small circular marks** that indicate unexpected events:

- **On the Life Line** – Illness, accidents, or sudden changes in life.
- **On the Head Line** – Sudden shock, trauma, or mental strain.
- **On the Heart Line** – Emotional shock, loss of a loved one, or betrayal.
- **On the Fate Line** – Unexpected financial loss or career downfall.

A **red dot** signifies danger, while a **black dot** may indicate **depression or long-term struggles**.

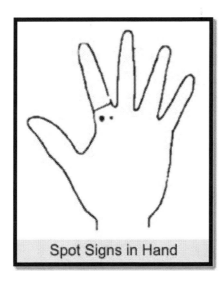
Spot Signs in Hand

5. TRIANGLE (△) – TALENTS & ACHIEVEMENTS

A **triangle** is a sign of special talents and intelligence:

- **On the Mount of Jupiter** – Success in leadership, education, or politics.
- **On the Mount of Mercury** – Business success and financial intelligence.
- **On the Mount of Saturn** – Deep wisdom, spiritual knowledge, and research skills.
- **On the Fate Line** – A major turning point in career or financial growth.

A **poorly formed triangle** may indicate **missed opportunities or wasted talent**.

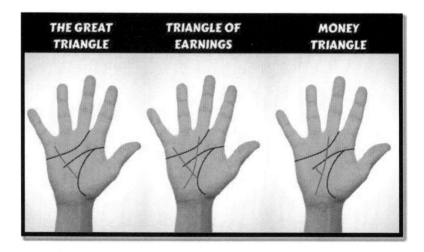

6. GRILLE (#) – BLOCKAGES & STRUGGLES

A **grille (mesh-like pattern of crisscrossing lines)** weakens the energy of a mount and suggests **confusion, challenges, or obstacles**:

- **On the Mount of Apollo** – Struggles in achieving fame or success in the arts.
- **On the Mount of Venus** – Excessive indulgence in desires, leading to problems.
- **On the Mount of Saturn** – Pessimism, isolation, or struggles.

If a grille appears prominently, **self-discipline and clarity of mind** are essential to overcoming challenges.

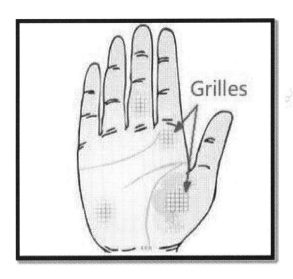

7. VERTICAL & HORIZONTAL LINES – STRENGTH & WEAKNESS

- **Vertical Lines** – Positive energy, success, and strength.
- **Horizontal Lines** – Negative energy, blockages, or delays.

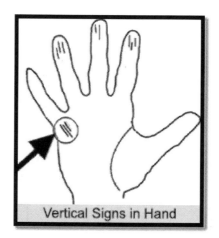

Examples:

- **A vertical line on the Mount of Apollo** = Success in arts or public life.
- **A horizontal line cutting the Fate Line** = Career struggles or obstacles.

8. THE RING SYMBOLS – SPECIAL MEANINGS

- **Ring of Solomon** (Curved line under Jupiter) – Wisdom and spiritual insight.

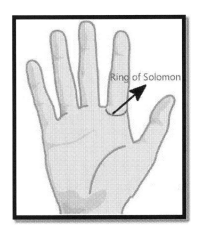

- **Ring of Saturn** (Semi-circle around Saturn finger) – Isolation, seriousness, and karmic struggles.

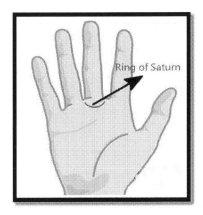

- **Ring of Apollo** (Curved line around the ring finger) – Difficulties in achieving fame or creativity.

- **Ring of Mercury** (Curved line around the little finger) – Emotional instability or dishonesty.

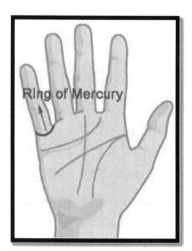

9. MOLES ON THE PALM – KARMIC SIGNIFICANCE

Moles on the palm are considered powerful symbols in palmistry. Their meaning depends on their **color, location, and size**.

GENERAL MEANING OF MOLES:

- **Black or Dark Brown Mole** – Challenges, obstacles, karmic debts.
- **Red Mole** – Energy, power, and hidden opportunities.
- **Light Brown Mole** – Mixed results, small obstacles with gradual success.

PLACEMENT MEANINGS:

- **On the Mount of Jupiter** – Ambition, leadership qualities, but possible arrogance.
- **On the Mount of Saturn** – Karmic debts, struggles, and possible financial instability.
- **On the Mount of Apollo** – Artistic success, but potential jealousy from others.

- **On the Mount of Mercury** – Business success but possible dishonesty in communication.
- **On the Life Line** – Health concerns or obstacles in early life.
- **On the Head Line** – Strong intellect, but risk of overthinking or mental stress.
- **On the Heart Line** – Intense emotional experiences, potential heartbreak.
- **On the Fate Line** – Unexpected financial gain or loss, depending on placement.
- **On the Palm's Center** – A balanced life, but with responsibilities.

Important Note:

- **A raised mole** (one that is slightly elevated) is more powerful in effect.
- **A large and dark mole** may indicate a stronger challenge or influence.
- **A tiny, light mole** has a weaker impact but still carries meaning.

10. TRANSVERSE LINES (HORIZONTAL LINES)

Meaning: Obstructions, delays, or obstacles in life.
Location: Found cutting across major or minor lines.
Effect: If deep and clear, they indicate strong challenges; if faint, they show temporary struggles.

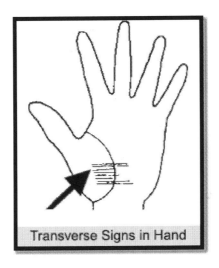
Transverse Signs in Hand

11. TRIDENT (THREE-PRONGED MARK)

Meaning: A sign of success, good fortune, and balanced energy.
Location: Found at the end of a line (Life Line, Heart Line, Fate Line, etc.).

Effect: Strengthens the line's meaning, bringing luck and prosperity.

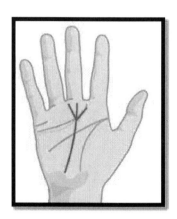

12. TASSELS (FEATHERED ENDINGS OF A LINE)

Meaning: Weakening of energy, confusion, or declining health in that area.

Location: Usually found at the end of the Life Line, Fate Line, or Head Line.

Effect: Indicates stress, loss of focus, or instability in life.

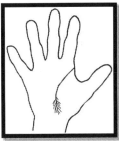

13. BREAKS IN LINES

Meaning: Sudden changes, interruptions, or transformation.

Location: Found in any major or minor line.

Effect: If the line continues after the break, it means recovery and new beginnings.

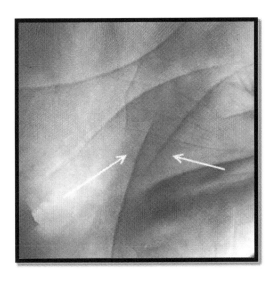

14. CHAINS (LINKED LOOPS IN A LINE)

Meaning: Uncertainty, struggles, and delays in that aspect of life.

Location: Common in the Head Line (indicating confusion) or Heart Line (showing emotional ups and downs).

Effect: Can mean health or emotional issues, but improvement is possible with effort.

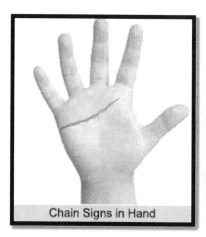
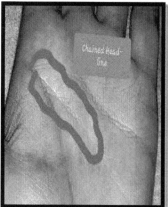

15. UPWARD LINES (BRANCHING UP FROM A MAIN LINE)

Meaning: Positive progress, success, and improvement.
Location: Found on the Fate Line, Life Line, or Heart

Line.

Effect: Shows personal growth, career achievements, and emotional upliftment.

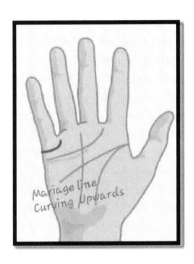

16. DOWNWARD LINES (BRANCHING DOWN FROM A MAIN LINE)

Meaning: Loss of energy, struggles, or negative influences.

Location: Found on the Fate Line, Heart Line, or Life Line.

Effect: May indicate depression, career struggles, or relationship challenges.

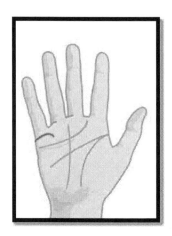

17. SQUARES (A BOX-LIKE SHAPE ON A LINE)

Meaning: Protection, safety, and divine blessings.

Location: Often found on the Fate Line, Life Line, or Heart Line.

Effect: A person will be protected from harm or recover from obstacles.

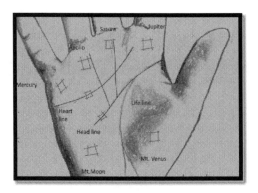

18. THE FISH SIGN IN PALMISTRY (MATSYA REKHA)

The **Fish Sign** (Matsya Rekha) is a rare and auspicious marking found on the palm. It typically appears as a small fish-like symbol, often located on the **Mount of Moon, Mount of Jupiter, or at the end of the Life Line or Fate Line**. This marking is associated with **spiritual growth, financial success, wisdom, and divine blessings**.

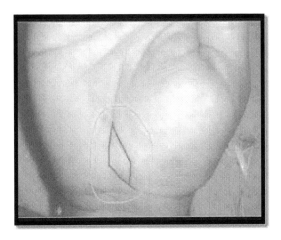

INTERPRETATIONS BASED ON PLACEMENT:

- **On the Mount of Moon** – Strong intuition, psychic abilities, and deep spiritual insight. The person may experience vivid dreams or prophetic visions.

- **On the Mount of Jupiter** – Great leadership qualities, success in politics, and a respected position in society.
- **On the Fate Line** – A strong destiny, luck in career, and unexpected financial gains.
- **At the End of the Life Line** – Indicates spiritual awakening, pilgrimage, or a divine calling later in life.
- **On the Mount of Sun** – Recognition, fame, and success in creative or artistic fields.

SIGNIFICANCE IN VEDIC PALMISTRY:

In **Vedic palmistry**, the Fish Sign is considered a divine blessing, indicating **protection from harm, good karma, and a strong connection to spirituality**. It is often seen in the hands of **religious leaders, sages, and highly spiritual individuals**.

19. THE SIMIAN LINE IN PALMISTRY

The **Simian Line**, also known as the **Simian Crease**, is a rare palmistry marking where the **Heart Line and Head Line merge into a single horizontal line** across the palm. This means the usual two lines are fused, creating a deep, uninterrupted line that runs straight across the hand. It is found in about **1 out of 30 people** and is considered both a unique and powerful sign.

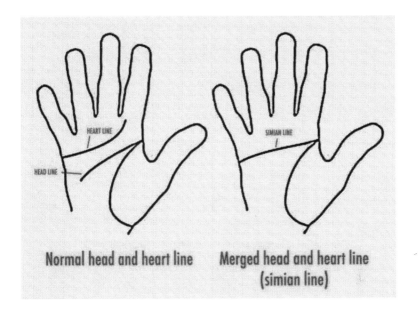

MEANING & INTERPRETATION

The Simian Line represents a strong **connection between emotions and intellect**. People with this line often experience **intense focus, deep emotions, and an all-or-nothing personality**. They may struggle with balancing logic and feelings but have **extraordinary determination** in whatever they pursue.

PERSONALITY TRAITS OF PEOPLE WITH A SIMIAN LINE

✔**Highly Focused & Determined** – When they set a goal, they pursue it with extreme dedication.

✔**Emotionally Intense** – They feel emotions deeply and

may have difficulty expressing them rationally.

✔ **Strong-Willed & Stubborn** – Once they make a decision, they rarely change their minds.

✔ **Spiritual or Scientific Thinkers** – Many spiritual leaders, geniuses, and researchers have this line.

✔ **Can Be Misunderstood** – Their direct nature may make them seem cold, but they often have deep emotions.

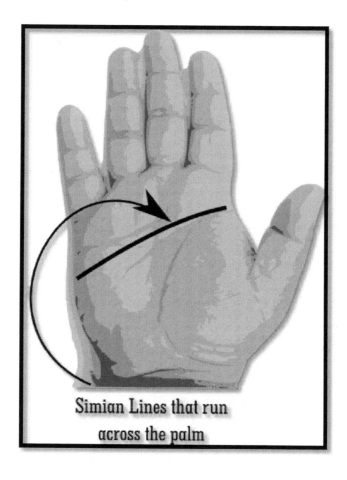

Simian Lines that run across the palm

POSITIVE & NEGATIVE ASPECTS

✓ **Positive:** Passionate, goal-oriented, strong intuition, deep thinkers, potential for great success.

✗ **Negative:** Prone to extreme emotions, difficulty in relationships, risk of mental stress or anxiety.

PLACEMENT ON ONE OR BOTH HANDS:

- **Simian Line on One Hand:** Indicates a strong but balanced personality.
- **Simian Line on Both Hands:** A rare occurrence, found in those with intense focus and sometimes extreme personalities. Many famous people, including scientists, monks, and successful business figures, have this marking.

SPIRITUAL & ASTROLOGICAL SIGNIFICANCE

In **Vedic palmistry**, the Simian Line is linked to **past-life karmic energy**, indicating a life of deep spiritual lessons. In **Chinese palmistry**, it is seen as a mark of **extreme success or struggle**, depending on how it is used.

FINAL THOUGHTS

Palm markings, including **crosses, stars, dots, islands, triangles, and moles**, provide **hidden insights** into a person's **life journey, strengths, weaknesses, and destiny**. They act as **indicators of past karma, life lessons, and potential challenges**. A skilled palm reader should analyze these markings **alongside the main lines, mounts, and hand shape** for a comprehensive reading.

CHAPTER 3: FINGERPRINTS & SKIN TEXTURE – HIDDEN CLUES IN YOUR HANDS

Palmistry is not just about lines and mounts; **fingerprints and skin texture** also reveal deep insights about a person's nature, thinking pattern, and destiny. The study of fingerprints, known as **dermatoglyphics**, has been used in both palmistry and modern psychology to analyze personalities and potential.

DERMATOGLYPHICS: THE STUDY OF FINGERPRINTS

Dermatoglyphics refers to the **patterns on the fingertips and palms** formed before birth. These patterns remain unchanged throughout life and serve as a **unique identifier** of a person's character and potential. Ancient palmists believed that fingerprint types indicate different levels of intelligence, creativity, and even karma.

Some key aspects analyzed in dermatoglyphics are:

- The **type of fingerprint pattern** (Loop, Whorl, or Arch).

- The **ridge count**, which measures mental sharpness and decision-making ability.

- The **skin texture**, which reveals emotional sensitivity and adaptability.

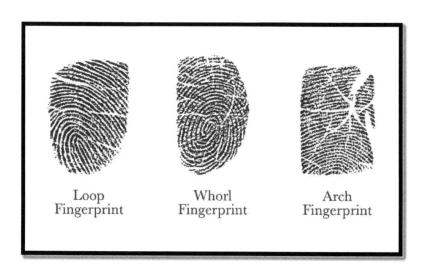

LOOP, WHORL, AND ARCH PATTERNS & THEIR MEANINGS

- ❖ **Loop Pattern (Most Common – 60-70% of People)**

  - **Personality:** Friendly, adaptable, easy-going, cooperative.
  - **Mindset:** Quick learners, but may struggle with deep focus.

- **Career:** Good in service-oriented and creative fields.
- **Spiritual Aspect:** Balanced karmic energy, able to connect with others.

- ## Whorl Pattern (25-30% of People)

- **Personality:** Independent, analytical, strong-willed, deep thinkers.
- **Mindset:** Logical, ambitious, but sometimes secretive or reserved.
- **Career:** Suitable for leadership, law, and technical professions.
- **Spiritual Aspect:** Strong karmic influence, destiny-oriented.

❖ **Arch Pattern (Rarest – 5-10% of People)**

- **Personality:** Practical, grounded, hardworking, cautious.
- **Mindset:** Slow to trust but highly dependable.
- **Career:** Best suited for stable professions like finance, security, and research.
- **Spiritual Aspect:** Indicates karmic lessons, overcoming struggles with patience.

❖ Special Patterns:

- **Tented Arch:** Highly intuitive and emotional people.

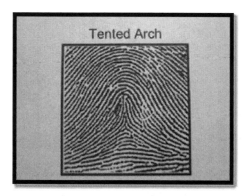

- **Double Loops:** Conflicted personality, dual-mindedness.

- **Peacock's Eye (Central Pocket Loop):**
Exceptional intelligence and rare talent.

HOW SKIN TEXTURE REFLECTS MENTAL & EMOTIONAL STATE

Palm skin texture can indicate a person's **mental agility, emotional resilience, and life approach**:

✅ **Soft & Smooth Skin** – Emotional, creative, artistic, sensitive to surroundings.

✅ **Medium Texture (Balanced Skin Type)** – Practical, balanced emotions, adaptable.

✅ **Rough & Coarse Skin** – Hardworking, strong-willed, physically active, resilient.

A person with **soft hands but rough fingertips** may be sensitive but highly determined. Conversely, someone with **rough hands and smooth fingers** might be a hardworking person with an unexpectedly creative side.

- **Palmistry Tip:**
  Fingerprints and skin texture **do not change over time**, so they give clues about your **innate personality rather than changing life events**.

PART 2: MASTERING THE ART OF PALM READING

CHAPTER 4: PALMISTRY AND CHAKRAS – THE ENERGY CENTERS IN YOUR HANDS

Palmistry is not just about physical features; it is deeply connected to **energy flow** within the body. Just like **chakras** (energy centers in the body), our hands store and emit energy, influencing our **thoughts, emotions, and destiny**. By understanding the connection between **palmistry and chakras**, we can balance our inner energies and unlock our full potential.

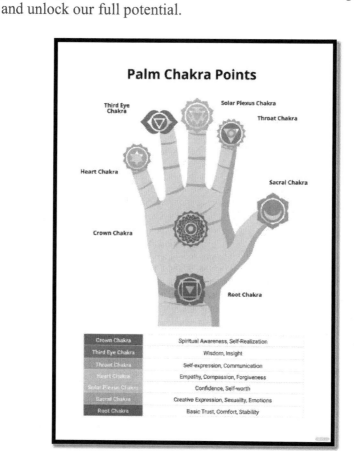

UNDERSTANDING THE SEVEN CHAKRAS IN THE HAND

Each part of the palm and fingers is linked to a specific chakra. When certain areas of the hand are strong or weak, they reflect **imbalances or strengths in that particular chakra.**

ROOT CHAKRA (MULADHARA) – BASE OF THE PALM

- **Represents:** Stability, survival, physical strength.
- **Palm Connection:** The **base of the palm** (near the wrist).
- **Signs of Strength:** Firm, strong base = good grounding, financial security.
- **Signs of Weakness:** Weak base or reddish skin = fear, financial instability.
- **Balancing Tip: Rub the wrist area** and practice grounding meditation.

SACRAL CHAKRA (SWADHISTHANA) – BELOW THE THUMB

- **Represents:** Creativity, passion, emotions.
- **Palm Connection:** Area below the thumb (Venus Mount).

- **Signs of Strength:** Well-developed Venus mount = passionate, expressive personality.
- **Signs of Weakness:** Flat Venus mount = low energy, lack of motivation.
- **Balancing Tip: Massage the Venus mount** and chant "Vam" mantra.

SOLAR PLEXUS CHAKRA (MANIPURA) – CENTER OF THE PALM

- **Represents:** Confidence, personal power, ambition.
- **Palm Connection: Middle of the palm (Mars influence).**
- **Signs of Strength:** Warm palm = confident, strong-willed person.
- **Signs of Weakness:** Cold palm = fear, lack of self-esteem.
- **Balancing Tip: Apply slight pressure to the palm center** and do breathwork exercises.

HEART CHAKRA (ANAHATA) – BELOW THE PINKY & RING FINGER

- **Represents:** Love, relationships, compassion.

- **Palm Connection:** Heart Line and area below the pinky.
- **Signs of Strength:** Deep heart line = loving and empathetic personality.
- **Signs of Weakness:** Faint or broken heart line = emotional wounds, difficulty expressing love.
- **Balancing Tip: Rub your palm near the heart line** and chant "Yam" mantra.

THROAT CHAKRA (VISHUDDHA) – MERCURY FINGER (LITTLE FINGER)

- **Represents:** Communication, truth, self-expression.
- **Palm Connection: Mercury finger (Pinky) and its mount.**
- **Signs of Strength:** Well-developed Mercury mount = strong communication skills.
- **Signs of Weakness:** Weak or curved pinky = difficulty in speaking up.
- **Balancing Tip: Massage the pinky** and do chanting exercises.

THIRD EYE CHAKRA (AJNA) – INDEX FINGER (JUPITER FINGER)

- **Represents:** Intuition, wisdom, insight.
- **Palm Connection: Index finger (Jupiter) and its mount.**
- **Signs of Strength:** Long and straight Jupiter finger = wise, intuitive leader.
- **Signs of Weakness:** Short or bent Jupiter finger = lack of confidence or insight.
- **Balancing Tip: Tap the index finger lightly** and focus on meditation.

CROWN CHAKRA (SAHASRARA) – FINGERTIPS

- **Represents:** Spirituality, enlightenment, higher self.
- **Palm Connection: All fingertips.**
- **Signs of Strength:** Rounded fingertips = spiritual awareness and deep wisdom.
- **Signs of Weakness:** Flat or blunt fingertips = lack of spiritual connection.
- **Balancing Tip: Hold your fingertips together** and practice silent meditation.

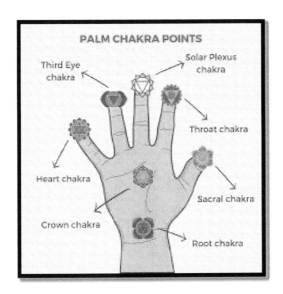

HOW TO ACTIVATE AND HEAL CHAKRAS USING YOUR HANDS

Hand Mudras – Specific hand gestures stimulate chakra energy. Example: **Gyan Mudra** (thumb and index finger together) enhances wisdom.

Palm Reflexology – Pressing different points on the palm helps clear energy blockages.

Color Therapy – Wearing specific gemstone rings or bracelets aligns chakras.

Reiki & Energy Healing – Holding the hands over different body parts heals chakra imbalances.

> 🔸 **Palmistry Tip:** If certain mounts or lines are weak, it may indicate a **blocked chakra**. By balancing these energies, you can improve your **health, relationships, and success**.

CHAPTER 5: THE SCIENCE VS. SPIRITUALITY OF PALMISTRY

Palmistry has long been a subject of debate, with some viewing it as a mystical art while others seek scientific explanations for its accuracy. In this chapter, we explore the contrasting perspectives of modern science and spirituality to understand how palm reading works on different levels.

HOW MODERN SCIENCE VIEWS PALMISTRY

From a scientific standpoint, palmistry is often linked to genetics and dermatoglyphics—the study of fingerprints and skin patterns. Scientists believe that the lines and ridges on our hands form in the womb and are influenced by our genetic code. Certain studies suggest that a person's hands can reveal information about their health, personality traits, and even neurological conditions. For example:

- Fingerprints and ridge patterns are unique to each individual and remain unchanged throughout life.

- Medical research has linked specific hand features to genetic disorders like Down syndrome.

- The structure of fingers and hand shapes may indicate hormone levels and brain development.

Despite these findings, mainstream science does not fully endorse palmistry as a predictive tool. Researchers argue that palm readings often rely on psychological factors, such as cold reading techniques and the Forer effect, where general statements seem highly personal.

THE ROLE OF INTUITION IN PALM READING

On the spiritual side, palmistry is considered more than just hand analysis—it is seen as a way to access a deeper level of intuition. Many palmists believe that reading hands is not just about lines but also about interpreting energy. Experienced palm readers develop a heightened sense of perception, allowing them to read subtle details that may not be immediately obvious.

- Intuitive readers often sense a person's energy and emotional state through their hands.

- The hand is believed to store past experiences, karma, and subconscious thoughts.

- Certain spiritual traditions link palmistry with past-life readings, aura reading, and astrology.

BRIDGING THE GAP BETWEEN SCIENCE AND SPIRITUALITY

While skeptics dismiss palmistry as pseudoscience, some modern researchers are exploring its potential as a diagnostic tool. Many holistic healers integrate palmistry with psychology, astrology, and energy healing to offer a more complete understanding of a person's life. By combining intuition with logical analysis, palmists can provide insightful guidance that resonates with both believers and skeptics.

Whether you approach palmistry from a scientific or spiritual perspective, it remains a fascinating practice that has been used for centuries to uncover hidden truths about human nature.

PALMISTRY VS. NUMEROLOGY VS. VEDIC ASTROLOGY

Palmistry, Numerology, and Vedic Astrology are three mystical sciences that provide insights into personality, destiny, and life events. Each has unique methods and principles, but they can also complement each other.

1. PALMISTRY: THE LANGUAGE OF THE HANDS

Palmistry, or chiromancy, studies the lines, shapes, mounts, and markings on the hands to reveal personal traits and future events.

KEY FEATURES:

- **Lines & Mounts:** Life Line, Head Line, Heart Line, and Fate Line indicate health, emotions, and career.
- **Hand Shapes & Fingers:** Four elements (Earth, Air, Fire, Water) define personality traits.
- **Markings & Symbols:** Special signs like stars, crosses, fish, and triangles represent strengths or challenges.
- **Practical Use:** Helps in self-discovery, relationship guidance, and career insights.

✓ **Best for:** Understanding personality, emotional tendencies, and major life events.

---

2. NUMEROLOGY: THE POWER OF NUMBERS

Numerology studies the vibrational influence of numbers on human life, derived from birth dates and names.

KEY FEATURES:

- **Life Path Number:** Represents life's purpose (calculated from birth date).
- **Destiny Number:** Based on full name, showing ultimate goals and ambitions.

- **Personality & Soul Urge Numbers:** Define expression and inner desires.
- **Repeating Numbers & Angel Numbers:** Certain patterns (111, 222) carry divine messages.
- **Compatibility & Predictions:** Used for marriage, career, and lucky dates.

✅ **Best for:** Discovering life purpose, lucky numbers, and personality traits.

---

3. VEDIC ASTROLOGY: THE COSMIC BLUEPRINT

Vedic Astrology (Jyotish) interprets planetary positions at birth to predict life events.

KEY FEATURES:

- **Birth Chart (Kundli):** Maps planetary positions to reveal strengths and life paths.
- **12 Houses & 9 Planets:** Each house represents a life aspect, while planets influence personality and events.
- **Dasha & Transits:** Planetary periods (Dasha) and movements (Transits) shape life changes.

- **Remedies:** Mantras, gemstones, and rituals counteract negative planetary influences.
- **Compatibility & Predictions:** Used for marriage, career, and financial forecasts.

✓ **Best for:** Deep life predictions, understanding karma, and determining favorable periods for success.

WHICH ONE SHOULD YOU CHOOSE?

Each system offers unique insights, and many people use them together for a complete analysis.

Feature	Palmistry	Numerology	Vedic Astrology
Focus	Hands & lines	Numbers & vibrations	Planetary positions
Predictive Accuracy	Moderate	Moderate	High

Best For	Personality & short-term predictions	Life path, career, and lucky numbers	Life events, karma, and remedies
Complexity	Easy to learn	Medium	Advanced
Requires Birth Date?	✘ No	✓ Yes	✓ Yes
Requires Birth Time?	✘ No	✘ No	✓ Yes (for accuracy)

CONCLUSION: THE BEST OF ALL WORLDS

- If you don't know your birth details, **Palmistry** is the best option.
- If you want to understand the deeper meaning of numbers in your life, go for **Numerology**.
- If you need in-depth predictions about life events, **Vedic Astrology** is the most powerful tool.

Many spiritual seekers use a combination of all three to gain a comprehensive understanding of their destiny!

CHAPTER 6: PALMISTRY CHARTS FOR ADVANCED READERS

Palmistry is a visual science, and advanced readers benefit greatly from **detailed charts** that map out different aspects of the hand. These charts act as quick-reference tools, allowing practitioners to identify hand shapes, mounts, lines, and special markings more efficiently.

1. ADVANCED PALMISTRY LINE CHARTS

- **The Life Line:** Variations such as chained, broken, or doubled lines and their meanings.
- **The Heart Line:** Different terminations—curved, straight, forked, and their impact on relationships.
- **The Head Line:** How its length and curvature influence intelligence and creativity.
- **The Fate Line:** Gaps, breaks, and their effect on career and destiny.

2. HAND SHAPE & FINGERPRINT CHARTS

- The **Earth, Air, Fire, and Water** hand shapes with their associated temperaments.
- **Fingerprints (Dermatoglyphics):** Loops, whorls, arches, and their deep psychological meanings.

3. SPECIAL SIGNS & SYMBOLS IN PALMISTRY

- **Crosses, stars, triangles, islands, and tridents**—their impact on different aspects of life.
- **Influence lines and parallel lines**—hidden messages about relationships and destiny.

These charts allow for **quick identification and deep interpretation**, making palm readings more structured and insightful.

CHAPTER 7: HANDWRITING & PALMISTRY – A SURPRISING CONNECTION

While palmistry deciphers a person's fate and personality through **lines and mounts**, handwriting analysis (graphology) reveals psychological traits through **strokes and pressure**. Both disciplines connect through the **neuromuscular system**, as the way a person holds a pen or moves their fingers is an extension of their inherent personality.

1. HOW HANDWRITING REFLECTS PERSONALITY

- **Large, bold letters** indicate confidence and ambition, often found in people with a well-developed **Mount of Jupiter**.
- **Small, delicate writing** suggests an analytical and detail-oriented mindset, linked to a prominent **Mercury Mount**.
- **Curved handwriting** (round letters) represents creativity, commonly associated with a **curved Head Line**.
- **Sharp, angular writing** shows decisiveness and strong willpower, often found in those with **long fingers and a strong Saturn Mount**.

2. FINGER FLEXIBILITY & WRITING PRESSURE

- **Flexible fingers** indicate adaptability, and these individuals often have **fluid, flowing handwriting**.
- **Rigid fingers** suggest a more structured personality, reflected in precise, uniform strokes.
- **Heavy writing pressure** signifies strong determination (similar to a deep, well-marked Fate Line).
- **Light writing pressure** shows sensitivity and a gentle nature (often seen with a soft-textured palm).

3. SIMILARITIES BETWEEN PALMISTRY & GRAPHOLOGY

- Both analyze **unconscious movements**—how fingers hold a pen is similar to how lines naturally form on the palm.
- Both reveal **personality traits**—confidence, creativity, ambition, and emotional sensitivity.
- Both can predict **life patterns**—consistent traits in writing or palm lines indicate recurring behavioral tendencies.

By combining palmistry and handwriting analysis, one can get a **holistic view of a person's character, emotions, and life path**.

CONCLUSION

Palmistry is more than just a method of fortune-telling—it is a powerful tool for self-discovery, personal growth, and understanding the hidden energies that shape our lives. Throughout this book, we have explored the deeper aspects of palmistry, from analyzing mounts and markings to understanding how palmistry connects with chakras, intuition, and even handwriting. By now, you should have a solid foundation to interpret the hands with greater confidence and depth.

HOW TO CONTINUE YOUR JOURNEY IN PALMISTRY

Learning palmistry is a lifelong journey. The more hands you read, the better you will become at identifying patterns, making accurate observations, and developing your intuitive abilities. Keep a palmistry journal, record your readings, and compare them over time. Practice with friends, family, and even strangers to sharpen your skills. Additionally, explore historical and modern palmistry texts to expand your knowledge.

PRACTICING ETHICAL & RESPONSIBLE PALM READING

With great knowledge comes great responsibility. As a palmist, you have the power to influence people's perceptions of their own lives. It is essential to approach every reading with honesty, sensitivity, and a positive mindset. Avoid making fear-based predictions, and instead, use palmistry as a tool to empower people, helping them recognize their strengths and navigate their challenges.

THE FUTURE OF PALMISTRY IN THE MODERN WORLD

While some still consider palmistry a mystical practice, modern research is beginning to uncover scientific links between hand features and a person's health, psychology, and genetics. As palmistry evolves, it will continue to bridge the gap between science and spirituality. Whether you use it for personal insight, career guidance, or spiritual growth, palmistry remains a fascinating and valuable skill that can unlock countless possibilities.

FINAL THOUGHTS

Your hands are a reflection of your journey—past, present, and future. They tell a story that is uniquely yours. By mastering the art of palmistry, you are not just reading lines; you are uncovering the blueprint of life itself.

If you wish to take your knowledge even further, **Volume 1** provides a strong foundation for beginners, and **Volume 2** has given you advanced insights. There is always more to learn in this vast and mysterious field. Keep exploring, stay curious, and let your hands guide you toward deeper wisdom and self-awareness.

May your journey in palmistry be enlightening and fulfilling!

A PERSONAL MESSAGE FROM THE AUTHOR

Dear Reader,

Thank you for embarking on this incredible journey into the world of palmistry with me. Writing this book has been a labor of love, fueled by my deep fascination with the secrets our hands hold. My goal has always been to present palmistry in a way that is easy to understand, practical to use, and deeply enriching for personal and spiritual growth.

Whether you are just beginning your palmistry journey with **Volume 1** or expanding your knowledge with the advanced concepts in **Volume 2**, I hope these books have given you valuable insights that you can apply in your own life and in the lives of others. Palmistry is not just about reading lines—it's about uncovering the unique story that every hand tells.

I encourage you to keep practicing, trust your intuition, and approach every palm reading with an open heart and mind. The more you explore, the deeper your understanding will become. If you ever have doubts, remember that the answers you seek are quite literally in your own hands.

If you found this book helpful, I would be truly grateful if you could leave a review on Amazon. Your feedback not only helps other readers find this book but also inspires me to create more content to support your learning journey.

Wishing you wisdom, clarity, and endless discoveries on your path to mastering palmistry!

Warm regards,
Nabanita Chakraborty

Made in the USA
Columbia, SC
28 March 2025